# COÖRDINATES OF YES

# COÖRDINATES

## OF

# YES

## POEMS

## JANÉE J. BAUGHER

*aha*dada

books

tokyo / toronto

General Editor: Jesse Glass
Layout and design: Joe Zanghi, Printed Matter Press
Cover design: Kristina J. Baugher
Cover art: "The Mother, 1659" by Pieter de Hooch (1629-1684)


editorial address:


3158 Bentworth Drive
Burlington, Ontario
Canada L7M-1M2


First Edition
Printed and Bound in Canada


ISBN 978-0-9812744-3-0

# ACKNOWLEDGMENTS

The author gratefully acknowledges poems in this book that have been published or accepted for publication in the following magazines and anthologies:

"Ballet der Spechte" in *Crate*; "Through the Looking-Glass, Part IV" in *Curiouser and Curiouser: Lewis Carroll Anthology*; "The Artist, as 'Incidental Person,'/Comments on His Book Tower –/His 'Skoob' Art (*Books* Backward)" and "Samson and Delilah" in *Ekphrasis*; "The Wounded Poacher" in *Ekleksographia*; "19th Century Cemetery in Gevrey-Chambertin, France" and "Les Tournesols et Vin" in *Enopoetica: A Collection of Poetry Inspired by Wine*; "Hôtel du Commerce, Paris" in *HA! A Humor Magazine*; "The Execution of Lady Jane Grey" and "To the Studios" in *Heliotrope*; "Souls Returning to Their Mortal Shells" in *Inertia Magazine*; "La Chambre de van Gogh á Arles" in *LitRag*; "Düsseldorf, Germany: Culminations" in *Main Street Rag;* "Portrait of Mona Lisa" in *Mona Poetica Anthology*; "At Juniper-Berries Lake/In Montagny-Les-Beaune, France,/I Consider Travel" in *Jump Start Anthology*; "Comfortable Distance" and "Notre-Dame de Paris" in *Quarter After Eight*; "Military Manoeuvres" in *StringTown*; "Eiffel Tower: View of Paris" in *The Pedestal Magazine*; and "Le Verrou" in *The Raven Chronicles*.

# POEMS ADAPTED FOR THE STAGE

*Hunger Between Here and Her* (a modern dance choreographed by Shellie Cash, with music composed by Jenny Bernard Merkowitz, based on the poem by the same title)

*immutable reflecting* (a modern dance choreographed by Shellie Cash, with music composed by William Brady Harrison, based on the poem "Ballet der Spechte")

*Meditation on Design* (a modern dance choreographed by Shellie Cash based on the poem by the same title)

*(the sunflowers and wine)* (a modern dance choreographed by Shellie Cash, with music composed by Jenny Bernard Merkowitz, partially based on the poem "Les Tournesols et Vin")

# Contents

## III.

## IV.

# I.

## Rinsing East

Over the Atlantic now, between
    plummet and sight:
    noctilucent clouds,
        perfect streak of sun-let,
        the unveiling of day.

Light fuchsia hovers under slate.
    Multiparous sky – perk sunshone,
    cadmium verve. Destined
        for watermark and landslide,
        resolute in this between-here.

In morning stark, me
    in a suit of mail –
    some spires of light
        ricochet off metal,
        some spires touch flesh.

## Venus mit dem Orgelspieler

*Venus with the Organ Player*
  – after the painting by Tiziano "Titian" Vecellio


Venus reclines on a divan, nougat
between red velvet canopy and red velvet
    cloth. Cupid peeks out from behind her,
and she turns to listen. At the divan foot,
    the organ-player. His hands on the keys,
he leans toward Venus, his scarlet coat
    into her cream essence. The metal
organ pipes tower over his shoulder.
    Mid-canvas: the honey landscape,
the country between them, between he


who loves and she who is loved. What
he must do to apprehend love. When
    he's successful, the expanse lessens.
He continues to lean and eventually
    Venus leans, too, until the landscape falls
behind them and the country between
    is theirs. And in that arrest, a new nation:
a place where red rises on its thread,
    Cupid claps in the wings and the organ,
through its ten effervescent mouths, sings itself.

## ALTE FRAU BEIM APELSCHÄLEN

*Old Woman Peeling Apples*
    – after the painting by Nicolaes Maes


Rationed sunlight over her shoulders and face. In a plain wimple,

    she peels yellow apples. On the window ledge,
    an opened Bible. A basket for the pared fruit

    sits to her left and a spinning wheel to the right.
    One escaped apple, defiantly more than an arm's length

    away on the clay floor. The plum skirt covers her legs and feet.
    The rounds rest on her lap where (despite arthritis) she

    deftly drops the unbroken ribbon of rind. Will it be
    preserves or pie? Perhaps neither. No origins, no sin.

Her aged, bulbous fingers part flesh from skin.

## Düsseldorf, Germany: Culminations

The summer festival tonight – he can't join us until later. The rest of us get there early. During our dinner of pizza and champagne, the Rhine quay packs tightly with those awaiting fireworks. Tonight I leave. We can't get him on his cell phone. I thought we'd never find each other between near and an unforeseeable far. Finally, he rings and we try describing our location – me in English directing Nicole in German. The hoard of people listening and amused or annoyed, I can't tell. Then I see him: *Kai, Kai.* He pushes through. The crowd cheers, parts, and in German someone cries "finally." When we reach each other I cannot conceive of ever letting go. Just then the boom boom boom of the artillery shells diffusing. The red pricks of light into a cinquefoil, their scintillation and crackling flares fusing out. We *ah* and clap through to the lingering haze of grey. He takes my hand – the sky still bursting umbels of lavender, blue, green, white – and leads me through the mob, and I forget how to say "excuse me." Smoke jelly-fish expunging – a matrix of flagella where light once stood. The cacophony and then everything's obtuse, an uncertainty of happened from invented. We arrive at the station with five minutes left. We hold on as long as possible. Although I ask him to go, he remains on the platform until my train blurs into night.

# Through the Looking Glass, Part I

– a pastiche of *Through the Looking-Glass* by Lewis Carroll

"Tickets, please. Show you ticket, child."
    The Guard was looking,
    first through a telescope,
    then a microscope,
    then an opera-glass.
    At last he said,
"You're traveling the wrong way....
Always speak the truth
– think before you speak –
and write it down afterwards."

        *"The pencil writes all manner of things that I don't intend."*

"Speak French when you can't think of the English for a thing –
turn out your toes as you walk – and remember who you are."

"So young a child,"
    said the gentleman sitting opposite to her,
"ought to know which way she's going,
even if she doesn't know her own name!"
    She, in that uncomfortable sort of age
    where things have no names.

        *"Must a name mean something?"*

# COUCHETTE

The dour conductor collects our passports:
        you're imperfectly valid with one,
        without one you're perfectly invalid.

"Shall we wake the German guy to work this cabin lock?"
        I say to the Australian woman on the lower berth,
        trying not to disturb the Chinese man next to her.

And as I write this down the other Australian
        asks what I'm doing. To "making poems" he says
        "influx." Tonight, the five of us sleep in motion

with the steady swishing-by of German air. Like on any
        other night, we simply take in what we can
        and convert it to what we need.

## HÔTEL-DIEU, BEAUNE, FRANCE

An elderly fellow sleeps on the entrance steps,
francs beside his face. No one will disturb them.

    Five hundred years of hospice.
    Thirty-one sickbeds align head-
    to-foot, pillows face the altar.
    Perpetual, thick white shams.
    Each bed: a tiny cloak room with
    resolute-red coverlets and walnut
    canopy. Stone floor and stoic chests,
    table and chair for each patient.
    Hooks for crucifixes.
    The church bell chimes six
    through eight lancet arch windows –
    portals not directly seen by the ill,
    mere rumors of sun.

Upon leaving, I find no sign of the old man
or his shiny coins.

## MIDDLE AGES APOTHECARY'S ROOM. IN EARTHENWARE:

solution cathéretique     ammoniaque liquide     eau d'orange

ether chlorque chloré     chloroform     alchoolat thériacal

poudre d'iris de flore     poudre de digital     sulfate de magnécie

vanille     poudre de camomille     poudre de belladona

citrate de fer     poudre roses de provin     gomme arabique

élixir de propriété     poudre de rhubarbe     colle de poisson

pierre divine     tartrate de potasse     cachou brut

## La Dame à sa Toilette

*The Lady at her Dressing Table*
— after the painting by an artist of Ecole de Fontainebleau


Her torso, naked luster.
       The onyx necklace,
a dive into cleavage.
       Amber hair pulled back.
A pearl to top the widow's peak.
       At her vanity she makes choices.
Strewn about the table, roses
       languishing blush and white.
They remind her:
       beauty wilts and thorns.
Love's red red rose which time
       alters regardless of how it
was plucked, watered,
       or steeped in light.

## PAINTED ON THE WINDOW, THE WORDS
## "TABAC" AND "BAR"
## SPREAD INVERTED ON THE TABLE INSIDE

At the bus depot in Dijon,
conspicuous with rudimentary French,
I purchase Marlboros and an Amstel.
The bartender inquires where I'm from;
four at the bar eavesdrop. "Etats Unis."
One old man asks about *black men*.
I respond, "Hommes noir sont mes amis."
Then, more French that I do not know.
The bartender asks a woman to translate
into English *mauvais*. Yet I know *bad* –
I comprehend the measure of things
black and white. So with my beer
and smokes, I bite my tongues
and move to the far back of the bus.

## At Juniper-Berries Lake in Montagny-Les-Beaune, France, I consider Travel

This morning, a young boy bikes to the opposite shore.
He casts his line. And waits.

> Water breezes west
> Birds, strident in the oak trees.
> Clouds meander east.

He reels in nothing. He climbs on his bike
and goes back the way he came.

> The wet line drips
> as he holds both pole and handlebars.
> Bicycle wheels: steadfast over pebbly earth.

The chain's slow, insistent squeak
trails him home.

## LES TOURNESOLS ET VIN

One hectare
        of sunflowers
                in red plastic hoods
        turn toward the sun.
I shed the red
        from one my height.
                I finger its yellow lips:
        spokes of sun
extending from its globe.
        I pluck a petal,
                and though I have
        no question of love,
I keep plucking.
        It takes one hour
                to lose count. Petals
        surround my feet.
Some scatter,
        some stick to toes.
                One I taste for luck,
        and consider
the vintners adding
        drops of this oil
                to their burgundy.
        As wine matures,
the more golden it grows.

A few of the blackened stones are eroded of dates.
Metal crucifixes and souvenir plaques. And as I stoop
to read inscriptions, a salamander scurries into dirt.
What does it know of food for worms or of the vineyard
across the road, fecund in lime and clay soil? In tending
to acres of Premiers Crus, the seasoned owner prunes his
vines. Year by year, these corpses' silent vantage: how
the mountains protect the crop, and the base's slope
sloughs precipitation. The molecules of burgundy
accumulating in their thin dead mouths.

# Border Crossing: France/Switzerland

Outside Hôtel-Chamoise,
the confidence of morning.
Static chair-lifts like birds on a wire.
Livestock bells through

certain mist.
Mist levitates
to mingle with a stratus
spiriting over Les Rousses lake.

The car crisscrossing a nebulous borderline.
Meadows dappled with Simmentals.
Evergreens in the foreground of
Jura Mountains. The irrepressible stars,

quite recognizable above
the road at my back.

**II.**

# EIFFEL TOWER: VIEW OF PARIS

Surely the stair-sweep knows
the homeless gather there at night –
the Arc de Triomphe, so stealth
in its threshold. Here, he's the only Parisian.
His broom swishes deftly contain
our careless litter. Five hundred metal stairs
to see Paris dense in white stone
as the Seine bobs its course. In the distance,
Versailles crowns proud,
thick in armor and woe. How well
the man knows the exact angle to use
on each bit of debris. He maneuvers
around us as we stare out, seeing
what it is we've come for.

## Hôtel du Commerce, Paris

Her Dostoyevsky room is the last one available in this town.
Madame Macabre, with furrowed brow and an offensive black mole.

From the common hallway, my hovel's door has no knob; only the lock
remains, contained within the aged wood. The sloped floor with buckling

putty-colored linoleum. The two single-paned dormer windows open in.
On the inside, the bolt and lock, a misfit. I must prop the plastic bidet

against the door for security. I go complain. In impatient French she yells
I'm too stupid to work the lock. Then, she refuses to give me shower access.

A part of me wants to spray-paint "condemned" on the façade and phone
the Better Business Bureau. I'd scream English vulgarities, but know

she's merely refusing to speak the language. Tonight, it's here or the street.
Back in my room, I notice calico-colored doilies on the bed stand and bureau

and an October-orange Afghan on the twin. So now, the other part of me
wants to share tea with this woman who uses lemon-scented

laundry detergent, and who can guide perfect, affable hospital corners.

# Le Tricheur à L'As de Carreau

*The Cheat with the Ace of Diamonds*
   – after the painting by George de la Tour


Cardboard soldiers poise
      between the cheat and the boy.
The boy is dressed in gilt satin
      with one peacock feather in his hat.
His cheeks have never known
      whiskers, or how a lady's pink lipstick
smudges off. Here in this brothel
      of red scent and franc, he sits green
at their table. So askew, the platform
      on which his arms rest.
He'll go home tonight
      wishing away that table
there, where aces are concealed,
      where aces conceal.

## La Chambre de van Gogh á Arles

*Van Gogh's Room at Arles*
   – after the painting by Vincent van Gogh


The Madame changes the linen weekly,
pale lemon-green sheets –
their hospital corners, rouge coverlet
On the lilac wall, portraits seem
uncertain of their hooks.
The wood floor, quite worn. The dressing table
(with bowl and pitcher), weary on its joints.
Above it, maelstrom in his mirror.
Through the one narrow window, yellow-primrose.
With cobalt-green, he's painted the panes shut –
the air in the room caves in on him.

# THROUGH THE LOOKING-GLASS, PART II

– a pastiche of *Through the Looking-Glass* by Lewis Carroll

"You've begun wrong…
the first thing in a visit
is to say 'How d'ye do?'
and shake hands."

"*I never put things into people's hands.
The first thing to do
is to make a grand survey of the country:
principal rivers, mountains and towns:
it's marked out just like a large chessboard.
I wouldn't mind being a Pawn –
a pawn goes two squares in its first move –
of course I should like to be a Queen, best.*"

## AFTER MEETING AN AMERICAN ARTIST IN PARIS
## WHO HADN'T BATHED SINCE THURSDAY

I wait in my hotel's courtyard. Often times
I first trust, then ask why. How. Chopin

plays from an upper room, the shower
chimes from my own. A man singing –

I cannot make out the language. Perhaps
it is the stranger in my room. This garden,

stark except for thirty containers of coral-
colored perennials, the white plastic table

and chairs and me – dressed in black and
writing more quickly now as I become

cognizant of the suspended water, and how
some days I seduce and other days I merely

fall into. The steam, still rising off his skin,
water drips from the ends of blond curls.

## Portrait de L'Artiste

*Portrait of the Artist*
   – after the painting by Vincent van Gogh


The one, sound ear.

                   Burnt sienna hair and beard.
          That stalwart sidelong stare. The background
                   swirls in aquamarine and amethyst,
             and suffuses onto your jacket and vest.
                       The white shirt buttoned to the top.

The cool hues overtaking, oscillating.

                   As you scrutinized the looking-glass,
          did you see the night you bled to death,
                a gunshot wound to the groin?

Arcs of paint. Imprecise circles.

                   The path on which you crutched was riddled,
                    riddled – paintings, chemical disparity.

The acuity

                   both salvaged and savaged.
         With it: maddened. Without it: maddened.
               Children taunting you,
           chasing with stones. Alone at night with your canvas,
                 you sensed them in every color.

The reason to chasm. Your shirt top, buttoned white.

## L'ATELIEUR DU PEINTRE, ALLÉGORIE RÉELLE

*The Painter in his Studio, Real Allegory*
  – after the painting by Gustave Courbet


Courbet sits mid-canvas in front of a nearly-completed landscape;
  he steadies the palette in one hand and paints with the other.
  Behind him,
  an admiring young boy and a nude model –
  her clothes heaped on the adobe-colored floor.

        Standing on his right: the affluent in fine frocks,
                their self-possessed postures.
        The area surrounding them, stamped in black.

Situated on his left, with gazes downcast:
the untidy and unclothed, beggars and peasants.
The wall behind them: a mosaic of beige-umber

and the shade of maps (azure, violet, lovat),
frayed at the center, ebbing on its geography.
While in task, the world rotates on its axis:

        no classes, no warrens, no frivolity. The pastoral –
            mountains, foliage, and expansive sky –
                balanced by its easel.

## Meditation on Design

Their hands lace and re-lace.
            Touch. Open.
Hands cleaved like
            scissors to the sky.
Nothing to refute
            the blue forever.
His and hers. Hands
            of stop and go,
hands ordaining self to self.
            Listen, if these two
are deep in knowing,
            the hands reflect this.
A design sure of itself, sure
            in its cupping *yes*.

## La Cathédrale de Rouen le Portail, Temps Gris

*The Great Door of Rouen Cathedral, Grey Day*
    – after the painting by Claude Monet

He perched at the hotel across the street.
Eight months in this vantage. How grey
those days of lonely painting. Fumes
of light, air of muse. What did he learn

about the precarious sun, the unshaping
of place? Such lightness of light –
that absence of light – solidifying his work.
Three bevelled stone thresholds. Centered,

the rose window and tracery. The spire
above it like a beacon. Tones of brown,
mauve, grey. His fluting of startling white.
What lay within this church? A reverie

known only to the blind? Did he ever enter
those portals – the ones I now see opening?

# THE TRAVELER IS A CHILD WITH STARS AND A FLOWER

– a pastiche of *The Little Prince* by Antoine de Saint-Exupéry


Grown-ups grow five thousand roses in the same garden
and they do not find what they are looking for.     The eyes are blind.
The flower stretches itself, timidly at first,
and then begins to push a charming little sprig towards the sun.


Words are a source of misunderstanding.
It is only with one's heart that one can see.
Sometimes, there is just enough room
for a lamppost and a lamplighter.
The flower continues preparing its beauty in its green chamber.
It is not the geographer's task to count the rivers,
the mountains and deserts.     Geographers don't record flowers.
They write of eternal things.     Flowers are ephemeral.
When one feels lonely in the desert, it is important to remember:
it is just as lonely among men; the wind blows them around.
They repeat whatever one says to them.
The child's flower is always the first to speak.


Listen to the stars. The stars are wells with rusty pulleys.
They pour drinking water.     It is like listening to light metallic sound.
Little bells changing themselves into tears.


Perhaps flowers have thorns out of spite.
Flowers are complex creatures.
Sometimes one is too young to know how to love.
When one is terribly sad, one loves sunsets.
The land of tears is so mysterious.


The child presses her nose against the window-pane.
All the stars, a riot of flowers. Only children know what they are looking for.
The stars are beautiful because of a flower one cannot see.

Over coffee – black with three sugars for him – the misanthrope spits *people take take take and expect you're welcome.* Under that peppercorn sky we walk to Jardin Luxembourg. His clothes loll from him as if he were a wire hanger. The garden's tidy shrubs, palm trees, red hibiscus. In the center, a shallow pond for small mechanized boats. From the bandstand: electric violin, marimba, bongos, oud. The music swells, people rising to what's primal: a certain thrumming, the insistent life. I take his hand. Afterwards, he buys Ganob's cassette for me. Around the garden's perimeter, a display of large aerial photographs. The photographer's shutter, click click: a shirtless Algerian plowing his wheat field, the sweat and brawn giving his skin the look of marble – his sable skin congruent against adobe. Click: the Nile's purposeful snaking – its slate-blue course through mud. And later at an Italian restaurant, we're befriended by five guys at the nearby table. Our anelli French to their rotelle English. The flowerman strolls by. A single red rose for me. But when we turn away, the vender reaches through the hedges to snatch it back. Later, at the hotel lobby his kiss of cigarette and haste. He heads back, 2 a.m.. Perhaps they had seen us, perhaps they were waiting for him. The five surround him. His airline tickets, francs, and passport, concealed in a money belt under his boxers. With his hands shoved deep in his pockets he pleads: *no fighting please, s'il vous plaît non combat.* That's when he feels it: in his pocket the sticky cellophaned cube. Paris Hash. He holds it up to them: *hasheesh, hasheesh?* They look to each other, decide *OK.* They leave him there on a night where one man exchanges harm for five highs, a woman sleeps in buttercup sheets, and somewhere in Africa a photographer does what he loves from a fantastic distance.

## LA PENSÉE

*The Thinker*
  – after the sculpture of Camille Claudel by Auguste Rodin

The marble square
appears unfinished.
His student's head
chaste white
protrudes from the top.
Under the stiff bonnet
dispirited eyes.
The chin rests on stone.
Inside, pleated petticoat pockets
conceal fist-sized mounds
of wet clay, her
clapped off nervous system,
the crushed aorta.

## Le Verrou

*The Bolt*
– after the painting by Jean-Honoré Fragonard

On the bedside table, the upended vase.
Next to it, a tempest of satin sheets and coverlet.

Discharged onto the mattress, a riotous sanguine canopy – howling red folds
assaulting white satin. The looming ten-foot door

its average-height knob, but to engage the methodically-situated lock
the man must extend his arm while on tip-toes. His other arm, stronghold

around the woman's waist. Her orpine-pearl dress still inflates behind her
from him having wrenched her up. His body thrust against

her incongruent pelvis. Her neck flung back, cocked on its axis.
Strands of blond hair undone. With one hand, she rams his chin from hers.

With the other, she attempts the bolt in vain. Tonight, in this room:
the coaxed-together like steel into casing, insisting-metal on metal.

Impelled into an interlocking scheme, she
with scattered flowers at the foot of the bier.

38

## PORTRAIT OF MONA LISA

> – after the painting by Leonardo da Vinci


The pink from head and neck
    has sunk into her hands –
one atop the other on the armrest.
    The eyes behind bulletproof
Perspex look everywhere.
    Nowhere.
The landscape: haunted austere abutment
    and a snaking dirt road leading
away.

O Mourning One,
    most of us will not know such woe:
the way you grew your child,
    the birthing hours on.
When she was just four…. Well,
    what we know of her death
is only your grief,
    Mother,
sfumatoed in black veil.

And so defiantly:
    a camera flash bulb.
This trips the mechanical partition.
    It lowers from a ceiling panel
over you. For one half hour:
    you, relieved,
there behind that impenetrable screen.
    And we
are spared your weeping.

## CONCESSION À PERPÉTUITÉ

> – in memoriam: Poet Élisa Mercoeur

What did I expect? A 165-year-old impeccable
Sainte-Anne marble monument with your poem
legibly inscribed? Your mother had it impressed
on the sarcophagus. But nothing's forever.

Letter by letter the poem vanishes, plaster-crumbling
so when I attempt this French by touch,
more erosion. I note what's discernible,
to know your poem by its parts, you by this stone.

> *Cette humble...*
> *Un souvenir...*
> *Peut-être...*
> *Ah! tout est froid...*
> *N'a pas même...*
> *Peut-être...*
> *Le bonheur est-il...*
> *Mais dans la nuit du monde...*

Moss has grown around the ledge, thick and clinging. Perhaps
from the inside you have read the poem to yourself, knowing those
words lost between air and tooth. In Père Lachaise soil,
the green ghoul spiders circumnavigate old bones.

O Mercoeur, have you climbed out the top of this tomb as weepers
look on? The cover is crooked enough for a girl's thin body.
Are you here, in this century where I breathe the sigh of you?
Your pieces which I may find, the path on which it's you I follow.

## DES GLANEUSES

*The Gleaners*
　　– after the painting by Jean-François Millet


Three black peasant women
　　　stoop in a reaped field.
　　　　　Dusk light, gradations of mauve,
lilac, blue – royal in royal opportune, for
　　　tonight they will feast.
　　　　　Each right hand reaches
stubbles of wheat. In the background
　　　harvesters on horseback
　　　　　vacate with their teams
and a year's supply. As for the women,
　　　white aprons folded
　　　　　in half about their waists.
From these pockets, stalks poke barren bellies.
　　　These three tonight to their
　　　　　shared home brimming gold.

## LE PRÊTEUR ET SA FEMME

*The Money-Lender and his Wife*
    – after the painting by Quentin (Metsys) Massys

According to one Flemish painter
the ingredients of wedded bliss:

one man and one woman; a single apple
on the shelf behind them; laid out on the table

a string of pearls, a mirror reflecting the outdoors,
a glass vase. See, he weighs gold coins

on the handheld scale while she studies her Bible.
His occupation and her avocation. Their arms

practically touch. The Bible's open
to an illustration of Mary and Baby Jesus.

As for Joseph, he's not in the picture.
I heard they never married.

## LES RABOTEURS DE PARQUET

*The Floorscapers*
    – after the painting by Gustave Caillebotte


Three kneeling in their black trousers.
In that isolation of motion,
    they could be railroad workers
or harvestmen. Young musculature,
the sheen of tanned backs. Each
    has his own metal scraper –
the outstretched labor hands. Curled
wood shavings on the floor around them.
    Near the hearth, a bottle of red wine, full
but for one glass-worth. It sits unsipped
beside the bottle. The middle worker,
    (wearing his wedding band) considers the wine.
The indivisible union between one man, one woman;
the tools by which we live, the coils we leave behind.

## Notre-Dame de Paris

My final night in Paris we meet at the bookstore across from the Notre-Dame – its south front side with rose window radial petals tracery and spire We buy falafel from a street vender beers for ten francs and walk across to the west two-tower facade – its entire face having been forced white with pressure-washing – to dine on the Seine quay Our backs to the twins and spire toward the sun tired over the river Because passers-by do not notice us no one cares to know our names or wonders if this will be our last meal or how when I'm saying good-bye it feels like I had just formed hello in my mouth Afterwards we get ice cream (white chocolate and cassis for me because he suggests it) We find another place to sit along the quay – the north-east side of the church still drab with soot and diesel And I think to myself maybe they'll get around to it someday years of Paris dropping into the Seine and that's when he tells me – how with ALS he'll likely be dead in five years dead before thirty and as I have lived barely thirty years all I can do is look out over the river and consider those rose windows and their transoms – how they're actually squared-off-intercepted-circles I say nothing Nothing when he rolls up his sleeves to expose truant muscles nothing Nothing even when he asks if we can hold each other tonight share a bed and holding on to what holds us Holding to that one moment when I look onto that cathedral unable to decide if I'm Beauty or Beast

# III.

## Through the Looking-Glass, Part III

– a pastiche of *Through the Looking-Glass* by Lewis Carroll

"Keep your head under the leaves,
and snore away there, till you know no more
what's going on in the world than if you were a bud.
Most times, there's no use in speaking.
The words go the wrong way."

> "When I use a word...
> it means just what I choose it to mean."

"The question is whether
you *can* make words mean
so many different things."

> "They've a temper, some of them –
> particularly verbs: they're the proudest –
> adjectives you can do anything with, but not verbs –
> however, I can manage the whole lot of them!
> Impenetrability! That's what I say.
> Wool and water: soldiers so uncertain on their feet."

## HOLLAND PARK YOUTH HOSTEL

Here, under one roof –
        from
        Tel Aviv,
        Jakarta,
        Kyoto... –
             these certain coördinates.

Bunkbeds stacked in threes
        on the
        alternating
        perpen-
        dicular.
             The bare beige walls, why they're

actually black, having soaked-up
        all
        flags'
        colors.
        Tonight,
             in white sheets and flannel duvets

fresh from the clothesline –
        all air
        struck
        and wind
        tucked –
             in purple plaid everyone of us dreaming.

## CHATTERTON

— after the painting by Henry Wallis of Poet Thomas Chatterton


How slight he looks, sprawled arsenic-dead across the bed.
His wavy chestnut hair soft as a boy's. Indigo knickers
and white stockings, one shoeless foot, the slipper hiding.
The open dormer window and the sun rising over London.
A small trunk brimming with torn scraps of his work-in-progress.
The meals he had to forgo for verse, the solitude he became.
Starved to simply create, devoured by fact: to eat required
publishing. Finished at seventeen! The apricot-red dress jacket,
discarded on a stool. On the small table, a divested brass candle holder.
Tattered bed linen, seams under pressure and him.... The creator
lives and dies by his work – the work's moot without him, yet
in its infinite permission, it's all that remains.

The left hand clutches the white blouse open. The right hand,
defeated on the floor in a rigor mortis fist of paper confetti.

# L'ESCARGOT

    – after the gouache-on-cut-and-pasted-paper by Henri Matisse


On his deathbed, Matisse
        arranged these gouache cutouts.
See, the blocks in their loose spiral
        touch: loden-tangerine-pumpkin-
tangerine-lemon -lilac- black -loden;
        so like one animal's ability
to go linear or coil back. Answer
        without, answer within.
His last work: a snail whose spiral-
        ling can never be tracked.

## OPHELIA

– after the painting by Sir John Everett Millais


The dress,
                    once so weighed with drink it downed you,
                                        inflates now around you.

Along the brook's shore:
                    nettles and stalks of reed.
Tethered lily pads                                        as you sneak by
            with the garland of poppies, violets, pansies, and daisies –
these you kept after giving the others.

Your ballooning white dress
                    stealing glints of light,
those soggy flowers
                            in colorful procession from pelvis to foot.

An enviable deathbed.

Willow branches
                    lean into your current,
                            letting down their vines in vain.

Auburn hair loosens
            and drifts in a blur around your head with
two parted lips,                                        two eyes open.

            Here, all unfolds without you,
despite the flowers you plucked
                    delicately, scholarly.

Now, your up-turned palms,

                                        empty.

# THE EXECUTION OF LADY JANE GREY

– after the painting by Paul Delaroche

The irrefutable luminance of her dress
is almost too much on the eyes.
If the executioner focuses on her nape,
the axe could hesitate there.
She feels the bole pressed to her cheek.
She becomes the stump of wood,
dead oak which once stood in sight
of stars. Stars quicken and quiver
there against perfect black.
The quest of black – from flesh of girl
to golden splinters. As for the axe,
the blade has its own agenda.

# EMACIATED FIGURINE BY ALBERTO GIACOMETTI

The sculptor
begins with
a metal
skeleton
then presses
clay to it.
Behold:
elongated
Everyman
rarefied and erect
on his plinth.
Cast, his surface
stays pitted.
Honest bronze,
extoller of light.
How much clay
to feign motion
depicts the metals
of our lives.
The indefensible
union of his fore-
boding matter.
He has not
toppled over
the edge. Look,
his arms check
so politely
at his side.

## COLD DARK MATTER: AN EXPLODED VIEW

– after the installation by Cornelia Parker

In a small garden shed, she scattered flotsam –
a bicycle tire, manual lawn mower, hair curlers, tin cans, toys –
and solicited the British army to detonate it.


The destructed pieces,
now threaded with fishing line
and tethered together. Amid
the smaller objects, she
hoisted the larger fugitives
(including the wood planks).
One 200-watt light bulb centers this vestibule-sized mobile.
Debris' shadows rib gallery walls.
Imploded articles pushed
from their original reference.
We each dwell in that clotted shed:
for all that we are, all that we do
patterns the universe.


Our infinite, immeasurable effect. The lines we draw
and the energy which vapors out.
Those shadow walls, ribbed gallery debris.

## TO THE STUDIOS

– after the painting by Frank Auerbach


Dollops of paint from tubes:
       the way out, the way in.
At times rust and brick
       are too much on the heart.
Scars grow whiter and moons
       hide on fingernails. Stare
at the thing to see it. See it
       by what surrounds it:
to paint the studio, paint
       what is not the studio.
Some days it is impossible
       to forget you're orphaned:
layers of paint dry on the floor.
       The eye's selective, and the skin's featured
only because of what grows inside.
       To know what can't be understood:
the way moths' wings seem
       chrome yellow (...) a tawny blur
is a naked model.
       Paint-to-canvas, layers on layers
and then scraping it back,
       scraping it back –
the excavation of you.

## BALLET DER SPECHTE

*Ballet of the Woodpeckers*
   – after the installation by Rebecca Horn

Horn spent a year in a sanatorium – illness from
        inhaling the fiberglass for a sculpture. Her art turned
against her, separating her church from state. To glimpse
        how it was, enter a room with eight large mirrors set in pairs

on four walls with mechanized woodpeckers intermittently
        striking the glass. Here, in this immutable reflecting,
your name escapes you. Simply hermetic so no matter where
        you turn: your image, image, your image, the infinitude

of it. You cannot find respite by merely blinding your eyes
        because of that pecking, peck, pecking.. a room of no silence.
tapping at the looking-glass looking back at you,, you,, you
        for something, anything tangible, no way, no,, no ways

to shatter the glass the body redoubling body into legions
        legions of lesions smaller and smaller & small while
you're caught there cinched at the seams and the birds
        pick at your threads with their little honed beaks... .

# THE LADY OF SHALOTT

– after the painting by John William Waterhouse


Faith leapt from the castle turret's window,
      and you to your brown prow.
You, in it for the journey, tired
      the way minutes merge until one day
you're thirty and still confined where Father
      bid you hold true. You had vowed
never to know Camelot: the air of morning,
      dew flirting on a cheek.
On walls and propped on easels,
      the mirrors permit the view of
out there. But when it's not enough,
      and your blindness
unbinds and your eyes sin against
      the man who is father and law,
to that small brown prow you go
      where even the crucifix
you cannot know.

# LONDON ARIA

The throng of weekenders daunts me
into settling for take-away; I return
to Holland Park Youth Hostel.
                    The park gates are closed to the public

for a nameless, ticket-only event.
I buy a Coke from the hostel's
vending machine and begin
                    climbing the stairs to my room.

That's when I hear it.
I return outside to the courtyard.
Through the cypresses:
                    the park's makeshift stage

and rows of tidy concert-goers.
The orchestra. The soloist. An opera!
I sit in the grass to eat my dinner.
                    But which libretto is this? I cannot

see her or the musicians... their notes
soaring from oblivion, for me
alone with my curry potato sandwich.

# AT THE BRITISH LIBRARY

Beowulf was neither man nor woman but legend
in the moon of ascent – unhanded by historians,
embraced by New Criticism, weighted in pyrite.

\*   \*   \*

Brontë sisters' writing table, splotched: blot of kin,
blood and black ink. One carved a C into the wood.
At the table, no hiding between apron strings.

\*   \*   \*

Handwritten edits from Joyce were done in pencil.
On the one occasion he attempted a fountain pen,
defeated Joyce was stained blue from mouth to knees.

\*   \*   \*

Woolf's favorite pen ran dry of its purple when the river
doused her clavicles – bones struck with wet and resign.
No turning back, just the river – diligent as its course.

## The Artist, as "Incidental Person," Comments on His Book Towers – His "Skoob" Art (*Books* Backwards)

– after the assemblage by John Latham

I merely accelerate erosion.
Dismembering books
by cracking their spines
and spray-painting them red.
Margins and words
bludgeoned to ash.
Hung on this wall:
mutilated texts tethered
together by a wire, open
to their turnable pages.
I find great comfort
in elemental changes,
like a swatter to a fly –
its infinite eyes seeing,
then not. Offended biblio-
philes, you are entitled
to love the words
beyond words.
As for me, I am
entitled to this.
My art is not
for making friends.
Your face now bruised
with anger, you wish
to do harm.
Here, you and I
are no different.

## CONDITIONS OF A WOMAN

> – after the installation by Armand Fernandez

In a transparent rubbish bin
objects from his wife's washroom:

> busted heel from a stiletto shoe
> wrap and cardboard from tampons
> a spent compact and cotton balls
> empty aspirin bottle
> relaxed balls of facial tissue
> an old lipstick soldier
> jar of depleted facial cream
> dried-up bottle of fingernail polish
> broken hair clip and Q-tips.

The used and left-behind, and the man who loves her for it –
he who sees what's embellished and squandered

in smoke and mirrors

a reflection insisting others are more fair.
Over the image she wastes her cosmetics;

with that heel

I imagine her smashing the glass.
And when her mate finds the pieces

she'll say:

beauty's in the eye, the eye, the eye.
It is no matter for art. Blood daggers in rain.

## MARES AND FOALS IN A LANDSCAPE

> – after the painting by George Stubbs, author of *The Anatomy of a Horse*

The Bay, Chestnut, and Grey huddle
under the oak tree near a lake.
Two foals' heads hidden on udders.
The three mares discuss this painter-

anatomist, how he would slash
a horse's jugular and add tallow
as preservative, the contained
unstrained quiet under skin,

broken in his dissection:
skin and fat from muscle, nerve
and vein from muscle, muscle from bone;
his stained hands rendering an exact

cartography of haunch to back to withers,
the dimpled breast, stately shoulder;
the way weight's often distributed
on three legs. But the horses prefer

the reverie of supposition, and they warn
their nursing foals to: "Run! run! run!"

## Samson and Delilah

– after the painting by Peter Paul Rubens


Delilah touches his brawny shoulders.
She tells herself she merely dreams.
No, he's not slumped in her lap, in deceit.
Hours before: rack of lamb and red wine,
her reaching over to touch his hair
and his taking her hand to kiss the lines.
The heart line's continuum, the life line
bifurcated at the center. And now,
her maid hovers over them. Candlelight
steadies. In the threshold, three soldiers.
The sickle-shaped locks falling away.

## GIRL WITH A WHITE DOG

   – after the painting by Lucian Freud


On a tawny sofa, the artist's first wife
pale in a green-gold robe. Its thick tie
settled on her lap. The English bull terrier
lies beside her, rests his chin where her thigh

meets knee. The robe's right shoulder
deliberately exposes her neck and full breast.
The haggard round is lifted by her right arm
(as she reaches over to cup the other breast).

Her unkempt hair in a part to the side.
Vacant-brown eyes, as large as her areola.
On her resting hand, the faint wedding band.
How often he attempted to climb inside

that robe with her protesting because
after so many hours painting he'd stopped
seeing her. She, in glaring asymmetry,
supporting the one peevish bust. He

screams at her to look alive. Their
sentimental-grey dog, quiet beside her.

## THE BATH

– after the painting by Pierre Bonnard


is an aerial view of
        the artist's wife in a bathtub.
Her brunette bob still dry.
        Her naked, pastel body:
mint-blue, teal-green,
        yellow-copper. And these
same hushed hues form
        the bath water. Osmosis
of her sympatico with water?
        Or perhaps it's the water's
insistence on her. Who
        can say which comes first,
or what's the artist
        without a modulus?
Art critics suppose
        she had tuberculosis or
an obsessive disorder. She
        endured cold water for him,
compromised spine, pruned digits.
        These are things he can't
with diligence consider
        in making the portrait right.
In the end, it is the artist alone
        with his cool colors and cold baths,
and a body that can permeate neither.

## NANTES TRIPTYCH

   – after the installation of three simultaneous video loops by Bill Viola


The middle video: underwater footage

of a clothed man plunging into water.
Sounds of breaking the surface. Living
submerged, treading from birth

to death. The left video: a woman squatting
on the floor gives birth. Breaths through
contractions, eeks of pain. The right:

a close-up of the artist's mother (bald head,
sunken-in eyes, a collapsed mouth) dying.
Deliberate breath sounds. During first breath

and last breath, only then are you in the know:
exacting life, exacting death. You swimming,
mingling bubble and buoyancy – your clothes

falling off. Even your weight is suspect.

They'd be brainless for a while because soon after death their brains were pureed with a metal rod and extracted through the nose. Brains regenerate. While conducting a ritual of anointment – scent of earth, scent of myrrh – they'd uncover their old preserved bodies. Uncoil strips of muslin from each limb and remove from the torso wood shavings, mud, sand. They could then easily slink in. Their internal organs were stored separately. The row of canopic jars could be pried open and the contents swallowed down: intestines, kidneys, pancreas, liver, lungs, spleen, stomach. The order's imperative. Hearts never leave the body. Often, the journey back took generations. Emerging from tombs, funerary amulets in their perfectly raisined hands.

# IV.

# Through the Looking-Glass, Part IV

– a pastiche of *Through the Looking-Glass* by Lewis Carroll

*"In our country there's only one day at a time:*
*it takes all the running you can do,*
*to keep in the same place."*

"I can explain all the poems that ever were invented:
they make their nests under sun-dials."

*"It's getting as dark as it can."*

"In a slow sort of country
put your hand down, and feel the ground –
you don't want to lose your name.
Did you go by the old bridge,
or the market-place?"

*"What does it matter where my body happens to be?"*

"Consider what a long way you've come today."

*"Tell me which road leads out."*

## THE FIRST NIGHT HERE I RECALL THE TRAIN RIDE, MY FORMING NOTIONS OF DUBLIN – MODEST GRANGES AS FAR AS EYES SEE

On this 400-year-old campus
       I dream of a distant train
on track. Greenlands
       like sweaters,
the greenest green
       of mind and bone.

I'm decades too late?

       Come, tuck me in bed.
Leave the drapes open.
       See this hourglass – watch
as I smash it, mindful
       as glass and grains
arrange in riot.

## MILITARY MANOEUVRES

– after the painting by Richard Thomas Moynan

A fifteen-member military band:
boys between six and eight years old.

Looking-on: a teenager with a basket of ferns,
three huddled young girls, a couple in sports attire

and old gentlemen. One boy carries a bayonet:
a tree branch with a red handkerchief.

Drums of milk crates and sticks. A trumpet
from a rolled-up newspaper. Coffee pot as bassoon.

Saucer pot lids as cymbals. Two wooden flutes. The band
pays no mind to the maestro with his hand-on-hip.

In bare feet and trousers rolled-up to the knee,
they travel down the sinkholed dirt road and pass

a Calvary trooper in his stepping-out uniform.
On the road, as they march and make music,

each boy inches closer to himself.

## The Wounded Poacher

– after the painting by Henry Jones Thaddeus

The cotter was paring parsnips when he banged at her door. The vegetables fell off her lap as she stood to answer. There slumped a young man with a rifle and two rabbits. His white shirt absorbing red. He stumbled in, sat down, and exposed the wound without bothering to yank the shirt tails from his wool trousers.

She leaned over him, dabbing a wet cloth on his pectorals. He fell into her, resting his head on her breast. His hat laid brim-side up on the clay floor next to an overturned chair. A small table with a bowl of water and bottle of alcohol. Underneath the table, a basket of parsnips.

At times, tripping on my shoestrings or over a misplaced root, I pray for someone to be home, there warming by the hearth and gently humming. To rest my agony upon a chest, there on the rampart where I crawl on my belly. How often I am the one rescued: insidious wounds, uncertainty at the door, the bereft pistol, and dead rabbits at my feet.

# DUBLIN IRELAND: AFTER MEETING A LOCAL MUSICIAN

Having ventured a quarter earth to see
    two halves moon timid behind cumulus,
I stroll along Dún Laoghaire's pier.
It could have been any other night –
    two strangers and evanescent Luna.
It's terrible, really, moments arrested
between knowing and not, the present
    and the journey back. His hand in mine
to the restaurant, quite closed. The owner
spots us, invites us in. Salmon walls,
    fresh linen, wafts of Indonesia. Talk of
Japanese poetry, *The Prophet*, racial tensions
in Dublin. Then, much later and so soon,
    that sober part of the morning seeing
what I've done and who I am. We stand
embracing for the time it takes to cross
    two countries, one ocean. How curious.
I could simply leave here, fall straight into
the Atlantic. O how anonymous
        that swim.

## STUDY OF A NUDE

    – after the painting by Francis Bacon


A small male stands full-bodied.
        His legs tightly together, firm
                on a thinly drawn white line:
        a pool edge or a metal bedstead,
it's too obscure to discern.
        His arms stretch over his head.
                Does he prepare to dive in?
        Or are his arms bound?
The lowered head
        fixes on the space below:
                smoky-purple,
        a semblance of his shadow.
How diffident this study of naked.
        Modesty has left him in effigy
                as he pauses before diving into it –
        breaching of bare into wake.

## PORTRAIT OF JOHN EDWARDS

*– after the painting of his heir by Francis Bacon*

Sitting in a chair, you
in your crudely pale features.
I can't make out your arms.
Perhaps you haven't any.
One leg is crossed man-like over
the other. On the floor, the region
where foot becomes toes is indistinct
– thick mauve oozes out
into an amoeba-shaped
puddle of spilt flesh. It
creeps to the chair leg
and clamps on as if
to pull itself back to you.
How long were you there
prior to your sloughing off?
Self-conscious of time, space
and the queuing of cells
– the ease by which one
can mew from the solid
to that certain pith of pink.

## SECOND VERSION OF TRIPTYCH
– after the painting by Francis Bacon


Three colossal canvases, three shape-shifters of contorted grey,
(each on its own pedestal), three mouths on necks.
In viewing this painting all your peripheral vision is red-magenta.

Two side panels: each figure presses against its canvas edge,
        the remaining space, mysterious in marooned maroon.
        The left: pageboy sprouted from a ream of peach-colored silk.
        The right: on the long-stretch neck, a human ear and inverted mouth.

The middle panel:
        most of the original khaki canvas remains.
        Its figure on tripod legs: protruding neck,
        cat ears and right-side-up mouth.

See this as a disease of the blood system of a woman you know well:
three mouths plot the story of infiltration, nuisance, and nuance of matter
and reason. An amalgam that not even a scientist can reach.

## Umbilicus

This altered state,
travel. Rivers unstrung,
reflections in wake.
Jazz on the tongue.
Alive in the un-know.
To thrive in this state
for a life time: crown
of thorns, the blood
I will run through.
And those who
know me know
nothing. Those who
know nothing don't
have it in for me.
And you, too, travel.
But you keep close
to ties that blind:
on a cell phone,
at the Internet Café.
Yet, home is relative.
Stepping barefoot
on ignited coals
the choice is yours:
to scar or to soar.

## ISLAND TO ISLAND

Amid crowns of heather,
I sit on a sheer, sure cliff

    of the Irish Sea. Far out,
    water as quiet as glass.

        A colony of gulls,
        a bobbing sea lion.

            That plunge into blue:
            frightening, inviting.

                Water-prisms
                reflecting, refracting

        with the assuredness
        of a lighthouse.

      Over this sea, wisps
      of nomadic clouds. I wait

    for something to happen –
    like how the ocean,

when it closes in on land,
turns a shy white.

# PORTAGING: THE FINAL DAY

## I. OPENING

How do the blind know of this Blind Garden?
By words of mouth, world in touch.
Opportunities for foliage and flora
in one hand, while fingering the plaque
with the other. Touch of petals,
smell of sun. Raised parchment,
the punched-out – translation of ink
into a language without accent.
After brunch we visit the garden,
and though we're both sighted,
I've never been so unseeing –
time pounding me on. Insisting.

## II. OPEN

This afternoon at The Porterhouse I wish
you would strum for me like that first night.
How shall I forget you, the way you slipped me up,
slipped me into your pocket how blind it was there,
blind to the derelict life. Loving.
This hour I'm vexed by bouts of sanity, how
the mirror pierces the eyes, eyes of blue and meadow
and nothing lovely except mere notion.
When you dedicated a song to me the C string broke.
I can't blame it, really, things undoing, unfettered.
The inevitability of parting. Vows to never never
never. The ticks that hail us on.

⇒

## III. Closing

It's evening and I'm drinking
so I can say this: I prefer the before –
before the detrition of fiction to fact.
During your first set last Sunday
we did not know. And now that I know,
I want it all back, a week knowing you,
walking on eyes. Shelled blind. To remain
strangers: take back the introductions,
stop the beers. The way undiscovered possibilities
don't disappoint. And because I can love, please,
that requiem and the way I found me in the lyrics:
*thousands of miles away, thousands. Away.*


## IV. Closed

2 a.m. and drunk and it's three hours until my flight.
I am ready. Me, the ancient tomb
of blind skin. As certain questions unravel,
I am poised now to collect them.
This has nothing to do with him.
It has to do with our bout between urns.
What steeps under skin? The cellular level
is deceptive. The blind in my garden
understand this is all one can give,
and have given it. Pressed between
the leaves, this is what I'll take away:
to love and to be loved, the blind must lead.

## At U.S. Customs

He asks: Do you have anything
            to claim? He means something
they should know about, a confession perhaps.
            Say, Jim Morrison's bust
or a first edition *Ulysses*. How to explain
            there are certain things
you cannot hold in your hand.

Yes, OK, he is asking
            about the contents of my pack:
a stolen wine key, a mousetrap
            with goat cheese and blood
still crusted in the spring,
            the carcass of an Irish bee.

No, he doesn't care about those.
            What *do* I have to claim?
I'm still standing here.
            I pull the backpack tight to my body.
It's all I have left.

## DRAINING WEST

Continent, what have you done?
    Awake all last night at a Dublin pub
    and today you spit me back.
        Must I now know my final destination,
        the conjugation of new tenses?

How odd the art of retrospection.
    On trains, relished in mobility,
    the ability to pass it all. Or to stop,
        those days laid out for the living –
        whetted under the skin.

The plane taxies now. Everyone's still.
    But when the lights flicker on,
    that unsettling tumult. And this is how
        we live our lives: intent on what's before us,
        fleecers of the present, this dusk hour,

renewed sky all melon and dove.

# NOTES

HUNGER BETWEEN HERE AND HER
> *Nutella,* a chocolate, hazelnut spread (especially delicious on bread).
> *Müsli,* a type of cereal usually served with cold milk.

BORDER CROSSING: FRANCE / SWITZERLAND
> *Simmentals,* a breed of cattle known for their white faces and reddish body with white markings.

HÔTEL DU COMMERCE
> *Hospital corners,* secure corners made by tucking in bed sheets at the mattress foot with a neat double fold.

L'ATELIEUR DU PEINTRE, ALLÉGORIE RÉELLE
> *Lovat,* a variegated color of green with shades of blues and greys.

COMFORTABLE DISTANCE
> *Ganob,* the name of a band from Egypt.
> *Marimba,* a musical instrument similar to the xylophone.
> *Oud,* a stringed instrument from North Africa similar to a lute.
> *Anelli,* a type of circle-shaped pasta the size of a pea.
> *Rotelle,* a type of pasta twice the size of anelli.

PORTRAIT OF MONA LISA
> *Sfumatoed* is the verb form of *sfumato* which comes from the Italian *sfumare,* meaning to tone down, to evaporate like smoke.
> *Perspex* is the British equivalent of Plexiglas.

NOTRE-DAME DE PARIS
> *Falafel,* patties of deep-fried, ground chickpeas served in a pita.
> *Cassis,* black currant.
> *A.L.S.* "Amyotrophic Lateral Sclerosis," a motor neuron disease.

OPHELIA
> Respectively, *Nettles, Poppies and Willows, Violets, Daisies,* and *Pansies* symbolize: pain, death, faithfulness, innocence, and thought or love in vain.

THE BATH
> *Sympatico* (noun), that which gets along well with others.

DUBLIN IRELAND: AFTER MEETING A LOCAL MUSICIAN
> *Dún Laoghaire* is a town twenty minutes south of Dublin.

## ABOUT THE AUTHOR

Janée J. Baugher was born and raised in Seattle and also lived in Nashville. She holds degrees from Boston University and Eastern Washington University. *Coördinates of Yes* is her début book.

# OTHER TITLES FROM AHADADA

*Ahadada Books publishes poetry. Preserving the best of the small press tradition, we produce finely designed and crafted books in limited editions.*

### Bela Fawr's Cabaret (David Annwn)                    978-0-9808873-2-7

Writes Gavin Selerie: "David Annwn's work drills deep into strata of myth and history,. exposing devices which resonate in new contexts. Faithful to the living moment, his poems dip, hover and dart through soundscapes rich with suggestion, rhythmically charged and etymologically playful. Formally adventurous and inviting disjunction, these texts retain a lyric coherence that powerfully renders layers of experience. The mode veers from jazzy to mystical, evoking in the reader both disturbance and content. *Bela Fawr's Cabaret* has this recognisable stamp: music and legend 'Knocked Abaht a Bit', mischievous humour yielding subtle insight."

### Age of the Demon Tools (Mark Spitzer)                    978-0-9808873-1-0

Writes Ed Sanders: "You have to slow down, and absorb calmly, the procession of gritty, pointillist gnarls of poesy that Mark Spitzer wittily weaves into his book. Just the title, *Age of the Demon Tools*, is so appropriate in this horrid age of inappropriate technology—you know, corruptly programmed voting machines, drones with missiles hovering above huts, and mind reading machines looming just a few years into the demon-tool future. When you do slow down, and tarry within Spitzer's neologism-packed litanies, you will find the footprints of bards such as Allen Ginsberg, whose tradition of embedding current events into the flow of poesy is one of the great beacons of the new century. This book is worth reading if only for the poem 'Unholy Millenial Litany' and its blastsome truths."

### Sweet Potatoes (Lou Rowan)                    978-0-9781414-5-5

Lou Rowan . . . is retired, in love and charged. He was raised by horse breeders and went to Harvard and thus possesses an outward polish. But he talks like a radical, his speech incongruous with his buttoned-down appearance. *Golden Handcuffs Review*, the local literary magazine that Rowan founded and edits, is much like the man himself: appealing and presentable on the outside, a bit wild and experimental at the core.

### Deciduous Poems (David B. Axelrod)                    978-0-9808873-0-3

Dr. David B. Axelrod has published hundreds of articles and poems as well as sixteen books of poetry. Among his many grants and awards, he is recipient of three Fulbright Awards including his being the first official Fulbright Poet-in-Residence in the People's Republic of China. He was featured in Newsday as a "Star in his academic galaxy," and characterized by the New York Times as "a treat." He has shared the stage with such notables as Louis Simpson, X. J. Kennedy, William Stafford, Robert Bly, Allen Ginsburg, David Ignatow and Galway Kinnell, in performance for the U.N., the American Library Association, the Struga Festival, and hundreds more schools and public events. His poetry has been translated into fourteen languages and he is a frequent and celebrated master teacher.

### Late Poems of Lu You (Burton Watson)                    978-0-9781414-9-3

Lu You (1125–1210) whose pen name was 'The Old Man Who Does as He Pleases,' was among the most prolific of Chinese poets, having left behind a collection of close to ten thousand poems as well as miscellaneous prose writings. His poetry, often characterized by an intense patriotism, is also notable for its recurrent expression of a carefree enjoyment of life. This volume consists of twenty-five of Burton Watson's new translations, plus Lu You's poems as they appear in the original, making this a perfect collection for the lay reader as well as for those with a mastery of Song dynasty Chinese.

**www.ahadadabooks.com**